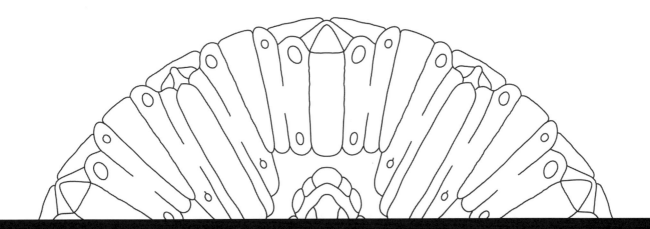

STRESS LESS COLORING™
MANDALAS

100+ COLORING PAGES FOR PEACE AND RELAXATION

Jim Gogarty, Founder of iHeartMandalas.com

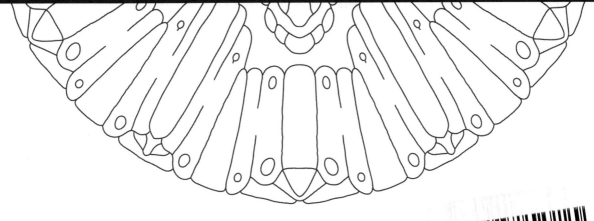

Adams Media
New York   London   Toronto   Sydney   New Delhi

Adams Media
An Imprint of Simon & Schuster, Inc.
100 Technology Center Drive
Stoughton, MA 02072

For information about special discounts for bulk purchases, please contact Simon & Schuster Special Sales at 1-866-506-1949 or business@simonandschuster.com.

The Simon & Schuster Speakers Bureau can bring authors to your live event. For more information or to book an event contact the Simon & Schuster Speakers Bureau at 1-866-248-3049 or visit our website at www.simonspeakers.com.

Interior images by Jim Gogarty

Manufactured in the United States of America

14 2023

Library of Congress Cataloging-in-Publication Data has been applied for.

ISBN 978-1-4405-9288-1

INTRODUCTION

Stressed out? Filled with anxiety? Looking for a way to clear your mind and add some creativity back into your life?

If so, coloring the more than 100 mandalas—ancient Indian Sanskrit for *circle*—in *Stress Less Coloring: Mandalas* will give you back your sense of balance. How, you ask? Coloring forces your mind to focus on the task at hand—filling in the mandala—which doesn't leave room for it to focus on stress. The reduction of these negative thoughts creates a sense of balance that's strengthened by the meditative quality of the mandala, which has been used for thousands of years to signify balance, unity, and a connection to all things in the universe. After spending just a short time coloring and letting your mind wander, you'll find yourself living a meditative life that's happier, healthier, and more in tune with the world around you.

To begin living a life that's more stress-free, take a look through the book and choose a mandala that speaks to you. Realize that some of these prints can be colored in quickly and some will require a little more time, effort, and relaxation to complete. Whichever mandala you choose is the one you are meant to color in, so don't worry about which print you've picked. Instead, relax; grab your pens, markers, or crayons; and open your mind to the meditative quality of the circle.

ABOUT THE AUTHOR

Jim Gogarty has had a passion for drawing for as long as he can remember, going from crayons to felt tips to today's digital pen. He began drawing mandalas in 2005 after a spiritual awakening during meditation. Since then, he has worked to turn this love for the symmetrical patterns into a career. He currently runs iHeartMandalas.com, where he brings these images to life, and he is the author of *The Mandala Coloring Book*. He currently lives in Hertfordshire, England with his supportive partner Susan and two children, Lillith and Charlie.